LETHAL COMPANY GAME GUIDE

Discover the Ultimate Strategies for Survival and Unlock the Secrets of the Indie Sensation with Secret Tips, Tricks, and In-Depth Guides for Beginners to Pros

George Hannon

Table Of Content:

Introduction

Welcome to the thrilling universe of Lethal

Company! In this guide, we'll delve into the

intricacies of the game, providing you with the

knowledge and strategies needed to navigate the

challenges and emerge as a formidable player.

Whether you're a newcomer seeking to

understand the basics or a seasoned adventurer

aiming to enhance your skills, this guide is

tailored for you.

Overview of Lethal Company

Lethal Company stands as one of the most
captivating indie games, offering a unique blend
of fun and horror in a solo-developed

masterpiece. With its rich depth and challenging gameplay, the journey through moons and encounters with diverse monsters make for an immersive experience.

Importance of Understanding Game Mechanics

Before embarking on your interstellar journey, it's crucial to grasp the fundamental mechanics that govern Lethal Company. From meeting quotas to facing unpredictable weather, every aspect contributes to the game's complexity.

This guide aims to break down these mechanics, empowering you to make informed decisions and conquer the challenges that await.

Whether you're interested in efficient scrap collection, mastering different moons, or strategizing against the diverse weather patterns, this guide has you covered.

Let's unravel the mysteries of Lethal Company together, so you can confidently step into this world and emerge as a seasoned explorer.

Chapter 1:

Getting Started

Game Basics:

Lethal Company offers an immersive

experience where your primary objective is to
fulfil your Quota by collecting scrap from
different moons. The company cares more about
the scrap than your survival, making each
mission a thrilling challenge.

Objective Overview: Understand the core
objective – achieving your Quota by collecting
scrap.

Planet Exploration: Navigate various moons, each with unique challenges, to gather resources. Always be ready to experience unexpected dangers.

Company Threats: Learn about the dangers posed by the company itself, including escalating Quotas and the pressure to deliver results.

Starting Quota:

At the beginning of your Lethal Company journey, you'll face limited resources and a modest Quota. Mastering the early stages is crucial for long-term success.

Managing Finances: Save credits initially, focusing on essentials and basic equipment.

Learn when to invest in tools that enhance your chances of survival.

Quota Progression: Grasp the concept of Quota escalation. As you meet targets, expect increased challenges. Balancing risk and reward becomes vital.

Essential Purchases: Explore the basics, such as acquiring flashlights or walkie-talkies, especially if you're a new player. These items ease navigation in the initial areas.

Early Game Strategies:

Surviving the early stages lays the foundation for your success in Lethal Company. Delve into effective strategies tailored for beginners.

Choosing Early Moons: Evaluate the three easy moons – Experimentation, Assurance, and Vow. Understand their difficulty levels and loot potential. Experimentation is recommended for newcomers.

Strategic Approaches: Develop strategic approaches for each early moon. Learn optimal routes, potential threats, and loot locations to maximise efficiency.

Gearing Up: Decide on equipment purchases based on your playstyle. Prioritise safety in the early game while building the foundation for more advanced strategies.

Controls Guide:

Understanding the controls in Lethal Company is crucial for effective gameplay. While some commands are intuitively displayed when interacting with items, others might remain undisclosed. Here's a comprehensive list of the current control scheme:

W, S, A, D: Movement

T: Default Push-to-Talk Key

Left Shift: Sprint

Space: Jump

Left Control: Crouch

RMB: Scan

LMB: Use equipped item

Scroll Wheel: Scroll between inventory items

G: Drop equipped item

1: Emote - Dance

2: Emote - Point

E: Interact

B: Move furniture in the ship

X: Store item in storage (While moving furniture)

R: Rotate furniture

Shift+H: Console/Developer Log?

Q / E: Flip page (Clipboard)

Z: Zoom in (Clipboard)

As the game is in Early Access, rebindable controls are not yet available. If you wish to customize your controls, consider using your peripheral software to bind keys or mouse buttons. Familiarise yourself with these commands to navigate, interact, and survive in the challenging world of Lethal Company.

Chapter 2:

Exploring Moons

*I*n Lethal Company, mastering the art of

exploring moons is crucial for survival and

success. Here's a breakdown of the various

moons you'll encounter throughout the game:

Early Game Moons

Experimentation

- **Description**: A beginner-friendly moon
  with lower loot but minimal threats.
- **Recommended Strategies:** Ideal for
  learning the game mechanics. Navigate
  carefully to understand moon dynamics.

Assurance

- Description: A middle-ground moon with more loot but increased dangers.
- Recommended Strategies: Suitable for players seeking a balance between risk and reward. Watch out for Eyeless Dogs.

Vow

- Description: The most challenging of the early moons with high danger and lower loot.
- Recommended Strategies: Approach with caution. Limited loot but a good test of advanced skills. Expect higher monster spawn rates.

Mid Game Moons

Offense

- **Description**: Tricky to navigate with high spawn rates for Coil-Heads. Similar loot to Assurance.

- **Recommended Strategies**: Coordination is key. Watch out for the challenging fire exit and potential ambushes by enemies.

March

- **Description**: A challenging moon with multiple fire exits and increased spawns.

- **Recommended Strategies:** Considered a trial rather than a primary loot source. Exercise caution due to the complex layout and higher difficulty.

Late Game Moons

Titan

- **Description**: Large loot pool with manageable difficulty, making it an excellent source of money.
- **Recommended Strategies**: Explore Titan for lucrative rewards, utilize the easily navigable entrance, and capitalize on potential ship spawns.

Rend

- **Description**: The most difficult late-game moon with low loot pool but high enemy spawn rates.
- **Recommended Strategies:** Communication is vital. Team coordination is crucial for handling the diverse range of enemies, including dogs,

forest keepers, Coil Heads, Jesters, and Brackens.

Dine

- **Description**: Challenging with a higher loot pool than Rend. Ship spawns may require extensive walking.
- **Recommended Strategies:** Plan your route carefully due to the ship's inconvenient locations. Beware of Forest Keepers and navigate strategically.

Mastering the moons is a key aspect of becoming a top employee in Lethal Company. Tailor your approach based on your team's skills and gradually progress from easier to more challenging moons.

Chapter 3:

Weather Challenges

*W*henever you embark on a lunar expedition

in Lethal Company, it's crucial to be aware of the
diverse weather effects that can significantly
impact your gameplay. Understanding these
effects is essential for survival, as each weather
condition alters the moon's environment,
introducing challenges that require unique
strategies.

Rainy:

Rainy moons introduce quicksand and mud
holes to the map. Navigating through these
hazards demands caution and awareness. If you

find yourself in quicksand or mud, move swiftly to escape before drowning. Always maintain stamina when exploring outside, and be attentive to any signs of slowing movement or slushing noises.

Storming:

Thunderstorms bring constant rain accompanied by frequent thunder strikes. Metallic objects are prone to lightning strikes, and a visual static buildup precedes each strike. Exercise caution with the items you carry and the loot you collect, as lightning can hit objects in your inventory, potentially affecting your ship and its power supply.

Flooded:

Persistent rain leads to water flooding the moon's surface, creating numerous pools that complicate navigation. Remember, your character cannot swim, so avoid drowning. Water levels may rise over time, making it challenging to spot water pools, particularly during the night. Leaving early is advisable to mitigate the risks associated with flooded moons.

Eclipsed:

An eclipse plunges the moon into permanent night, allowing monsters to spawn immediately. This creates a high-risk environment right from the start. Consider avoiding eclipsed moons, as the challenge level is significantly elevated with creatures roaming freely in the darkness.

Foggy:

Thick fog blankets the moon, making navigation difficult for all but the most familiar with the map. While the fog limits visibility, be aware that some creatures, like the Forest Giant, remain unaffected. Choosing moons where such creatures spawn might pose increased risks due to reduced visibility, making it harder to evade potential threats.

Understanding and adapting to these weather effects is pivotal for lunar survival. Evaluate the risks associated with each condition before choosing your next destination, and ensure your strategy aligns with the challenges posed by the moon's atmospheric conditions.

Chapter 4:

Items and Strategies

*I*n Lethal Company, mastering the effective use

of various items is crucial for survival and success. Understanding the strengths and weaknesses of each item can significantly enhance your gameplay. Here's a detailed guide to the items and strategies that can make the difference between success and failure.

Battery Powered Items

Walkie Talkie

- **Description**: A fundamental communication tool with diverse applications.

- **Strategies**:
    - Assigning a player as the monitor for enhanced coordination.
    - Creative uses such as marking paths or synchronising movements.

Flashlight

- **Description**: Illuminates your surroundings, but choose wisely between standard and Pro-Flashlight.
- **Strategies**:
    - Pro-Flashlight recommended for extended battery life.
    - Beware of battery drainage and utilize sparingly.

Boombox

- **Description**: A morale-boosting item with a potential for distraction.
- **Strategies**:

- Luring monsters using the Boombox's sound.
- Marking entrance locations for easy navigation.

Zap Gun

- **Description**: A weapon with scanning capabilities and stunning effects.
- **Strategies**:
  - Effective teamwork combining Zap Gun with other weapons.
  - Unique uses like stunning Forest Giants or disrupting Jester performances.

Jetpack

- **Description**: A heavy item for transporting loot, but handle with caution.
- **Strategies**:

- Mastering jump launching for efficient use.
- Understanding the risks of prolonged use to avoid explosions.

Melee Weapons

Shovel

- **Description**: A lightweight melee weapon with no lightning attraction.
- **Strategies**:
  - Safe and versatile option for dealing with enemies.
  - Ideal for clearing spider webs and speeding up Hygroderes.

Stop Sign

- **Description**: A heavier version of scrap weapons, with lightning risks.

- **Strategies**:
  - Caution advised due to the risk of lightning.
  - Selling for a shovel recommended in most cases.

Yield Sign

- **Description**: A heavy and less practical melee weapon.
- **Strategies**:
  - Classified as F Tier, generally not recommended.
  - Consider selling for better alternatives like a shovel.

Infinite Items

Lockpicker

- **Description**: A valuable tool for exploring, especially in locked areas.
- **Strategies**:
  - Placing strategically to unlock doors efficiently.
  - Awareness of its noise attracting monsters like coilheads.

Extension Ladder

- **Description**: A light and versatile tool for navigating terrain.
- **Strategies**:
  - Mastering shortcut knowledge for effective ladder use.
  - Ideal for accessing tough-to-reach places.

Radar Booster

- **Description**: A device providing additional visibility in the compound.
- **Strategies**:
  - Placing boosters strategically for monitoring key locations.
  - Effective use on stormy planets for managing Eyeless Dogs.

Stun Grenades

- **Description**: Single-use items with potential alternative uses.
- **Strategies**:
  - Stunning enemies for a quick getaway.
  - Utilizing casings to remove mines, offering unexpected utility.

Single Use Items

Stun Grenades (Really, this time)

- **Description**: One-time use items with stunning effects.
- **Strategies**:
  - Pausing Jester's songs and escaping from pursuing enemies.
  - Specific uses against certain monsters for tactical advantages.

TZP-inhalant

- **Description**: An expensive stamina-boosting item with side effects.
- **Strategies**:
  - Effective for carrying multiple items but use wisely.
  - Understanding and managing side effects for optimal results.

Chapter 5:

Ship Configuration and Upgrades

*T*he ship in Lethal Company serves as your

command centre, equipped with a terminal, radar, launch control, and various elements crucial for your survival. Understanding how to optimize your ship's layout and make strategic upgrades can significantly impact your gameplay.

Ship Configuration Tips:

- Press B to change the layout of equipment in the ship.

- Use X to store selected equipment in the storage, especially props without a current purpose.
- Rotate selected equipment to enhance organization and accessibility.

Optimizing Ship Layout:

- Keep the terminal close to the radar and launch control for efficient coordination.
- Position the light switch near well-lit areas, enhancing visibility, especially around the radar.
- Note that items like the take-off lever, cameras, door buttons, battery charger, clothesline, and the random air tank are fixed and cannot be moved.

Ship Upgrades:

1. Loud Horn (Cost: 150)

- A loud signal horn audible throughout the facility.
- Pull the lever for a short blast or hold for a prolonged one.
- Strategic use can clear paths, particularly when the entrance is blocked by creatures like eyeless dogs.
- Useful for assisting the team in entering the ship safely or facilitating an escape.

2. Teleporter (Cost: 375)

- Allows teleporting teammates back to the ship.
- Select a player on the radar and press the button after lifting the glass cover.

- Inventory drops upon teleportation, so use judiciously.
- Ideal for rescuing teammates in dire situations, such as being stuck or close to death.
- Can be initiated before a teammate is in immediate danger to save them.

3. Inverse Teleporter (Cost: 425)

- Similar to the Teleporter but teleports you to a random location within the facility.
- Causes players to drop items upon teleportation.
- Stand near it to be randomly teleported.
- Multiple players can use it simultaneously, each ending up in a different location.

- Rumors suggest that placing a new radar booster may influence teleportation proximity.

Understanding ship configuration and wisely choosing upgrades can be pivotal in navigating the challenges presented by Lethal Company's moons.

Chapter 6:

Effective Strategies

*I*n Lethal Company, mastering effective

strategies is crucial for survival and success.
Whether you're navigating moons, facing
challenging weather, or dealing with menacing
monsters, employing the right tactics can make
all the difference.

Communication and Teamwork

Communication is the cornerstone of success in
Lethal Company. Coordinating with your team
can be the key to overcoming challenges and
meeting quotas efficiently.

Here are some communication and teamwork strategies:

- **Assign Roles**: Designate specific roles within your team, such as a monitor for staying onboard, scouts for exploring, and defenders for protecting the group.

- **Walkie Talkie Coordination**: Utilize walkie talkies effectively. Monitors can guide explorers, share important information, and strategize without being physically present.

- **Emergency Signals:** Establish clear signals using ship horns or other agreed-upon methods to communicate danger, successful loot collection, or other critical situations.

Map Navigation Tips

Navigating the moons can be complex, but a well-versed team can turn challenges into opportunities. Consider the following tips for map navigation:

- **Memorise Key Areas**: Familiarise yourself with essential locations on each moon. Knowing where the entrance, exits, and key loot spots are can save valuable time.

- **Path Planning:** Plan your routes and memorize them. Efficient navigation prevents unnecessary encounters with monsters and helps meet quotas faster.

- **Use of Radar Boosters**: Place radar boosters strategically to enhance visibility on the ship's monitor. This aids navigation and allows monitoring of key locations.

Monster Encounter Strategies

Encountering monsters is inevitable, but facing them with the right strategies can tip the scales in your favor. Consider the following monster encounter strategies:

- **Coordinated Attacks**: Coordinate attacks on monsters using weapons like the Zap Gun. Stun monsters to allow safe passages or create opportunities for loot retrieval.

- **Forest Keeper Tactics**: When dealing with Forest Keepers, use stun grenades strategically. Stunning a Forest Keeper can save a teammate from being eaten.

- **Dealing with Night Creatures**: On moons with an eternal night (Eclipsed), be prepared for constant exterior spawns.

Focus on countering threats like Forest Keepers efficiently.

Utilizing Moon-Specific Tactics

Each moon presents unique challenges, requiring tailored approaches. Be aware of moon-specific tactics:

- **Adapting to Weather**: Adjust your strategies based on weather conditions. For example, in Stormy weather, use radar boosters effectively to locate Eyeless Dogs.

- **Lunar Environment Awareness:** Consider the characteristics of each moon, such as quicksand on Raining moons or the vastness of Titan. Adapt your gameplay to navigate these challenges.

- **Exploiting Moon Features:** Some moons have advantageous features, like easy-to-navigate entrances on Titan. Exploit these features to maximise loot collection and quota fulfilment.

By integrating these effective strategies into your gameplay, you and your team can become formidable employees in the challenging world of Lethal Company. Always adapt your approach based on the specific conditions of each moon and work collaboratively to outsmart the company and its deadly environment.

Chapter 7:

Advanced Gameplay

Terminal Commands

*I*n the advanced realm of Lethal Company,

mastering terminal commands can significantly enhance your efficiency. This section delves into various commands that empower you to navigate the game interface more swiftly and execute advanced functions.

Terminal commands in Lethal Company and their respective functionalities:
You must understand that the Terminal is not just a static interface; it's your beacon in the

darkness. To make the most of its features, you need to understand the fundamentals.

Go to the Terminal and hit 'E' to engage, whether in space or on a planet. Importantly, it's recommended to make purchases in space, and you can exit the Terminal anytime with 'TAB'.

Now, let's explore the numerous commands the Terminal provides.

Commands And Their Effects:

- **Help**: Here's where you begin, this command shows you a thorough list of accessible commands.

- **Moons**: The "moons" command provides essential information about available moon locations and their respective hazard ratings. Understanding this data is vital for planning your missions and gauging the risks involved. Additionally, specific commands like "[moon name] info" and "[moon name] route" offer in-depth details and navigation assistance.

- **Store**: The "store" is a command you'll frequently use to purchase crucial equipment for your missions. This command allows you to access a variety of items, ship upgrades, and decorative elements. Learn the syntax for purchasing items like a pro.

- **Bestiary:** Explore the "bestiary" command to gain insights into the various monsters you might encounter from their behaviours to weaknesses. This resourceful tool provides information that remains accessible even after death, offering valuable knowledge to enhance your monster encounters. You can use specific commands like "[monster name] info"

- **Storage:** "Storage" is one of the Lethal Company commands you may or may not use often. To arrange and adorn your ship, employ this command for rearranging furniture.

- **View Monitor:** Pivotal for monitoring teammates' positions and activities, this command enables or disables the main monitor's cam, offering a strategic view of players in the lobby.

- **Switch [Player name]:** This command allows you to switch the main monitor to a specific player, aiding in opening secure doors and teleporting corpses back to the base.

- **Ping [Radar booster name]:** The 'Ping' command emits a noise from the radar booster making it a valuable tool for situational awareness in the vast landscapes.

- **Scan:** The "scan" command is a powerful tool for assessing the number and total value of items located outside the ship or on the map. This information is crucial for efficient resource management during missions.

- **[Unique identification code]:** The 'Unique Identification Code' command deactivates turrets and opens secure doors.

- **Sigurd:** For lore enthusiasts, the 'Sigurd' command unveils log entries that offer insights into the mysterious narrative of Lethal Company.

- **Other:** The 'Other' command serves as an entry point to extra features, offering a variety of actions to enhance the flexibility of your gameplay.

And those are all the current Terminal commands you need to know in Lethal Company. Mastering these Terminal commands will empower you to navigate the complexities of Lethal Company with precision and effectiveness.

Once you become familiar with these commands, you'll seamlessly integrate them into your gameplay, ensuring a smoother and more successful journey beyond the safety of the Company ship.

Always remember to adapt commands based on the specific moon, item, or situation.

Controller Information

Understanding the nuances of using controllers in Lethal Company can provide a different gaming experience. Explore the intricacies of controller settings, button mappings, and how to optimise your gameplay with different controllers.

How To Set Up Controller Support:

Lethal Company offers an engaging gaming experience with partial controller support, allowing players to use controllers like Xbox, Nintendo Switch Pro, and PlayStation 5 controllers. While not all actions are controller-friendly, players can still enjoy the game with this feature. Follow these steps to enable controller support:

Enabling Controller Support:

1. **Connect Your Controller:**
    *   Plug in or connect your controller via Bluetooth before launching Lethal Company.

2. Compatible Controllers:

- Although Xbox Controllers are officially supported, players can also use Nintendo Switch Pro and PlayStation 5 Controllers.

Controller Bindings:

Gameskinny provides specific bindings for each supported controller:

1. Lethal Company Xbox Controller Buttons:

- Interact/Grab: Y
- Drop item: B
- Browse through items you're currently holding: D-pad left to right

- Power on item (Walkie-talkie):
  D-pad down
- Use item in hand: RT
- Scan the vicinity: RB
- Inspect item: LB
- Move furniture on ship: X
- Exit Terminal: +

2. Lethal Company PlayStation Controller Buttons:

- Interact/Grab: Square
- Drop item: Circle
- Browse through items you're currently holding: D-pad left to right
- Power on item (Walkie-talkie):
  D-pad down
- Use item in hand: R2

51

- Scan the vicinity: R1
- Inspect item: L1
- Move furniture on ship: Triangle
- Exit Terminal: Start

3. Lethal Company Nintendo Switch Pro Controller Buttons:

- Interact/Grab: X
- Drop item: B
- Browse through items you're currently holding: D-pad left to right
- Power on item (Walkie-talkie): D-pad down
- Use item in hand: ZR
- Scan the vicinity: R
- Inspect item: L
- Move furniture on ship: Y

- Exit Terminal: Start

Steam Overlay for Remapping (Optional):

- **Remapping Controls:**
  - Some buttons may not be usable, and emoting is currently unavailable.
  - Use Steam Overlay by pressing Shift+Tab to remap controls during gameplay.
  - Ensure in-game Steam settings match the provided image.

Future Updates:

There may be full controller support in the future as Lethal Company progresses through its early access phase. Stay tuned for updates and improvements to enhance your controller gaming experience.

Downloading and Installing Mods

Take your Lethal Company experience to the next level by exploring the world of mods. Learn how to safely download, install, and manage mods to introduce exciting new elements, challenges, or enhancements to your gameplay. Modding Lethal Company can enhance your co-op experience and introduce exciting changes to your gameplay. Follow these steps to safely install mods:

Prerequisites:
Before proceeding, it's advisable to make a backup of your game files.

Although Lethal Company modding is relatively safe, having a backup ensures you can revert to the original version if needed.

1. Navigate to your Steam library and find Lethal Company.
2. Right-click on the game and select "Manage," then choose "Browse local files."
3. Copy everything in this folder to a separate location to create a backup.

Getting Ready:

Ensure your game version is up to date. Right-click on Lethal Company, go to "Properties," and check under "update" for the latest app ID (1966720) and build ID (12681469).

Installing Mods:

Step 1: Install Thunderstore Mod Manager

- Visit the Thunderstore Mod Manager website and download the installer.
- Install the Thunderstore Mod Manager at your preferred location.
- Open the manager and use the search bar to find "Lethal Company."
- Create a profile, allowing you to manage different mods for varied gameplay experiences.
- Select the created profile and ensure the correct game directory is chosen in settings.

Step 2: Install BepInExPack

- In Thunderstore Mod Manager, click on "Get mods" in the left sidebar to open the store.
- Search for "BepInExPack" – a vital Unity mod framework for Lethal Company modding.
- Install BepInExPack. This framework is essential for enabling mods in the game.

Step 3: Install Additional Mods

- In the Thunderstore Mod Manager, explore available mods by clicking "Get mods."
- Choose mods based on your preferences and click "Download with dependencies" during installation.

Step 4: Launching Lethal Company with Mods

- Click the blue "Modded" button at the top right of Thunderstore Mod Manager to start Lethal Company with mods.

- Congratulations! You've successfully initiated Lethal Company with mods. To play an unmodded session, launch the game directly from Steam.

Additional Notes:

- To uninstall or disable a mod, click the arrow next to it in Thunderstore Mod Manager and choose the respective option from the drop-down.

Explore different mods to customize your Lethal Company experience.

Monsters Spawn Chances On Different Moons

Dive deep into the statistical aspects of the game. Gain insights into the spawn chances of different monsters on various moons. Understand the probabilities and factors that influence the appearance of these formidable foes, allowing you to adapt your strategies accordingly.

Here's a breakdown of the spawn probabilities for various monsters on different moons:

Experimentation:

- Bunker Spider: 26%

- Hoarding Bug: 12%

- Bracken: 5%

- Snare Flea: 23%

- Hygrodere: 14%

- Thumper: 7%

- Spore Lizard: 15%

- Ghost Girl: 0.5%

Assurance:

- Bunker Spider: 22%

- Hoarding Bug: 24%

- Bracken: 4%

- Snare Flea: 29%

- Hygrodere: 9%

- Thumper: 7%

- Spore Lizard: 4%

Vow:

- Bunker Spider: 13%

- Hoarding Bug: 21%
- Bracken: 27%
- Snare Flea: 20%
- Hygrodere: 9%
- Thumper: 3%
- Spore Lizard: 6%
- Coil Head: 2%

Offense:

Similar to Assurance:

- Bunker Spider: 22%
- Hoarding Bug: 24%
- Bracken: 4%
- Snare Flea: 29%
- Hygrodere: 9%
- Thumper: 7%
- Spore Lizard: 4%

March:

- Bunker Spider: 21%
- Hoarding Bug: 12%
- Bracken: 19%
- Snare Flea: 13%
- Hygrodere: 5%
- Thumper: 25%
- Spore Lizard: 3%
- Coil Head: 3%

Rend:

- Bunker Spider: 15%
- Hoarding Bug: 12%
- Bracken: 18%
- Snare Flea: 11%
- Hygrodere: 2%
- Coil Head: 24%
- Ghost Girl: 7%

- Jester: 24%

Dine:

- Bunker Spider: 15%
- Hoarding Bug: 11%
- Bracken: 6%
- Snare Flea: 12%
- Hygrodere: 9%
- Coil Head: 12%
- Ghost Girl: 4%
- Jester: 15%
- Spore Lizard: 4%
- Thumper: 11%

Titan:

- Bunker Spider: 13%
- Hoarding Bug: 8%
- Bracken: 14%
- Snare Flea: 12%

- Hygrodere: 4%
- Coil Head: 13%
- Ghost Girl: 6%
- Jester: 15%
- Spore Lizard: 3%
- Thumper: 12%

Understanding these spawn chances will empower you to anticipate and strategize for encounters with different monsters on each moon. Tailor your approach based on these probabilities to enhance your chances of survival and success in the game.

Conclusion

Congratulations, Lethal Company Explorer!

You've delved into the depths of this indie gaming sensation, and now it's time to reflect on your journey. Let's recap some key points and offer a bit of encouragement:

Recap of Key Points

- **Understanding the Basics**: You've grasped the fundamentals of Lethal Company, from meeting your quota to navigating the intricate moon landscapes. Remember, success often starts with a solid foundation.

- **Moon Exploration**: The game's moons hold secrets and challenges. Early, mid, and late-game moons each present unique opportunities and risks. Your choice of destination can significantly impact your success.

- **Weather Challenges**: Facing the elements is an integral part of your mission. Whether it's rain, storms, floods, fog, or an eternal eclipse, adaptability is key. Prepare for the unexpected and conquer the moons under various conditions.

- **Strategic Item Use:** Your arsenal is vast, from battery-powered devices to melee weapons and beyond. Choose your tools wisely, and always be ready to adapt your strategy based on the situation.

- **Effective Teamwork:** Communication and collaboration are your greatest assets. Whether using walkie-talkies, radar boosters, or teleporters, working seamlessly with your team can turn the tide in your favour.

- **Advanced Tactics:** As you progress, delve into advanced gameplay elements like terminal commands, mod installations, and understanding spawn chances. Become a master of Lethal Company by exploring its intricacies.

Encouragement for Players

As you continue your journey in Lethal Company, remember that each challenge is an opportunity to learn and grow. Embrace the thrill of exploration, the camaraderie of your team, and the satisfaction of meeting your quota.

Whether you're a seasoned player or just starting, the universe of Lethal Company is ever-evolving.
Don't be afraid to experiment with different strategies, adapt to changing circumstances, and, most importantly, have fun. In this vast and unpredictable gaming landscape, you have the chance to become the ultimate employee.

So, go out there, gather that scrap, conquer the moons, and show the world what it truly means to be the best in Lethal Company!

Safe travels, and may your scrap collection endeavours be both thrilling and rewarding!

www.ingramcontent.com/pod-product-compliance
Lightning Source LLC
Chambersburg PA
CBHW062248290526
45794CB00006B/2458